TODAY
AND
TOMORROW

TODAY

AND

TOMORROW

Embracing God's Plan for Your Future

GARRETT BOOTH

BVB

Bold Vision Books
PO Box 2011
Friendswood, Texas 77549

Copyright 2016 © Garrett Booth

ISBN # 978-0-9978514-3-4 (pb)
ISBN # 978-0-9978514-6-5 (cl)

LCCN # 2016-9604-16

Written with Karen Porter

Interior design—*k*ae Creative Solutions
Cover design—Josh Pierce

Published in the United States of America.

Bold Vision Books
PO Box 2011
Friendswood Texas 77549

Dedication

To my family,

Andrea, Lauren, and Austin

—you make the journey fun and exciting.

And to my church family

The people of Grace Houston

—your faith and faithfulness are inspiring
and encouraging.

Table of Contents

Introduction

*It's never too late for
a fresh start.
~Anita Agers Brooks*

It is always exciting to begin. It may be a new day or a new year, a new career or job, a new school or a new relationship. We love a fresh start. The blank page is ready for us to write our new story or paint our new masterpiece. Our past doesn't matter. Our future stretches before us.

Never think that it is too late for you. God gives you a new day every twenty-four hours. The Bible says, "*Through* the Lord's mercies we are not consumed, because His compassions fail not. *They are* new every morning; Great *is* Your faithfulness" (Lamentations 3:22-23).

You may wonder if there is hope for you, too. My desire is for you to know how much God loves you, and that even in the worst parts of your past, He was working to bring you to this moment.

The concepts in this book are centered on a story in the Old Testament found in the Book of Joshua.

God's people were on the way to pursue the promise He had given them. The journey moved them out of slavery and set them free by God's power. They left Egypt and crossed the Red Sea, moving toward the promise of God. But because they were afraid and unbelieving, the nation wandered in the wilderness for forty years.

A long time.

The first generation who had been slaves died, and now their children moved into the Promised Land to claim God's future for them. Moses was the leader of the first generation. Joshua is the leader of this new generation, and he leads them to the Jordan River. At that place, they stand ready to leave the past behind and embrace the future. To move from one place to another. They had heard stories of the Promised Land, and now they are ready to cross the river and make the stories their reality.

Perhaps you have also come to a place where you need to leave your past behind and march into your new life—your new destiny with God. The answers to your questions are found in God's Word, and from the example of the nation of Israel, we will discover what to do next.

Israel faced obstacles as they entered the land. There were walled cities to conquer. There were battles to fight. There were enemies to vanquish. There was also the presence of God. Every step of the way, He was helping. He was guiding. He was leading.

God is with you as you march into your future, too. He has woven your past into your present, preparing you for the future. I pray this book will help you discover how to prepare today for the tomorrow that God has planned for you.

I believe in you, and I believe in our mighty God who will help us all find new strength, mercy, and joy for the journey.

~Garrett Booth

Section 1

Preparing Today

*By failing to prepare, you are
preparing to fail.*
~Benjamin Franklin

Not being prepared can cost you. It's true
in relationships, business opportunities, and every part of
life. I learned this lesson again not too long ago in a unique
way. My wife Andrea is a talented athlete. She can play
any sport with very little practice or training. It is kind of
disgusting, really. She and I were playing basketball one
afternoon. As we played, I got distracted by something in the
gym just as she passed the ball to me. It was a line drive—a
cannon-shot of a pass. I turned around in time for the ball
to hit me full-force right in the face. She claimed it was an
accident, but I think we all know the truth. My bloody nose
that day reminded me that there is always a cost to not being
prepared.

Being prepared is important in every aspect of life, especially spiritually. We can be prepared for what God wants to do next in our lives. We can be ready to make the decisions that God wants us to make. And those decisions will affect our future. Dr. Ben Carson, who grew up in a single-parent home in a poor neighborhood became one of the world's greatest pediatric neurosurgeons and a U.S. presidential candidate, said, "Great things were going to happen in my life, and I had to do my part by preparing myself and being ready."

Preparation means to equip yourself and precondition yourself for what might happen next. Preparation requires us to cultivate strengths and overcome weaknesses. It calls us to train and condition our mind, soul, and spirit. We are preparing today for what we will be tomorrow.

> *You had better live your best and act your*
> *best and think your best today; for today is the*
> *sure preparation for tomorrow and*
> *all the other tomorrows that follow.*
> *~Harriet Martineau*

We mistakenly think that success in life just happens. That it's about being at the right place at the right time. And we believe some people are lucky and some people are not. The truth is that luck has nothing to do with it. I agree with artist Henry Hartman, who said, "Success is when preparation meets opportunity." The question is not will you have opportunities, the question is will you be prepared when they come.

Preparation is an important part of your journey with God. Preparation is a biblical concept. God prepared the garden for Adam and Eve (Genesis 2). Abraham prepared an altar (Genesis 22). Joseph prepared for the famine (Genesis 41). Moses prepared the tabernacle (Exodus 25-28). Esther prepared for one year to see the king (Esther 2). John the Baptist prepared the way (Matthew 3). Jesus is preparing a place for us (John 14).

In the first section of this book, I want to talk to you about getting prepared *today* for God's *tomorrow*. When God's people entered the territory called the Promised Land, God brought the nation out of slavery to this new future. Joshua, their leader, said, "Sanctify yourselves, for tomorrow the Lord will do wonders among you" (Joshua 3:5). In other words, Joshua told the people to "get prepared."

Together, we will discover how to get prepared for our future. We will cover four ways to prepare: prayer, perspective, position, and participation. Preparation begins with prayer—communicating with God who loves us unconditionally. Preparation requires us to change our view of life—having a God-perspective and knowing that He is in our future. And preparing for God's future compels us to take a stance that is ready, anticipating the blessings and provision of our Father.

So let's prepare to get prepared.

Chapter 1

Preparing in Prayer

The most important conversation you'll ever have.

*True prayer is neither a mere mental exercise
nor a vocal performance.
It is far deeper than that—it is a spiritual
transaction with the
creator of heaven and earth.*
~ Charles Spurgeon

MY SON AUSTIN LOVES LEGOS! He is 12 now and for the last number of years, my son has asked for Legos® for every birthday and Christmas. He loves to build fire stations, city buildings, and superhero hideouts. One time he had his eye on a Lego set that was recommended for kids 12 and up. Austin was only 6-years-old at the time, and so I knew that it would be a big challenge for him. He wanted the set so badly that I gave in and bought it. True to form, as soon as we got home he raced to his room and started building. When my son is in "building mode," it is all he thinks about. Eating can come later. Sleep is unnecessary. He is laser-focused on the project. After 30 minutes of struggling with a set that was clearly too difficult for him, I heard him call out across the house. "Daaaaaaadddddddd, I need your help!" I was there in a flash to help him conquer the Lego construction project. All he needed to do was call out to me.

Austin believed two important facts about his father that day. These facts are also true of our Heavenly Father. Austin believed that his father *could* help him, and he believed that his father *would* help him. The same is true of God. Prayer is calling out to our Heavenly Father when we get in over our head, believing that He *can* help us and He *will* help us. I wonder how many times I've missed out on His help because I did not call out through prayer.

Prayer is simply having a conversation with God. We tend to overcomplicate what prayer is all about. To begin praying, we do not need a class, a seminar, a conference, or a seminary course. If we can have a conversation, we can pray. Prayer is that simple, and all of us can do it. Preparing for tomorrow begins with connecting with God—and that preparation starts with prayer.

We will never travel beyond the limits of our prayer life. As Joshua and God's people faced the beginning of a new chapter in their lives, they were prepared in prayer. Joshua's leadership of the nation was based on his development of a personal prayer life with God. As a young man serving Moses, Joshua was the only person who journeyed with Moses up Mount Sinai to seek God (Exodus 24:13). Joshua's deep commitment to prayer caused him to stay at the tabernacle and pray even after everyone else had gone home (Exodus 33:11). God established the tabernacle for His people to learn how to communicate with Him. Connecting with God through prayer was a centerpiece of life for His people. He taught His people to pray in preparation for receiving His promise.

Think about this incredible idea—you can communicate one-on-one with the God of the universe. He is omnipotent, meaning He is all-powerful. He is omniscient, meaning He is all-knowing. He is omnipresent, meaning He is everywhere. He created everything, including you. God spoke the world into being, and He holds it all together.

When David reflected on this thought, he wrote, "When I consider your heavens, the work of your fingers, the moon, and the stars which you have set in place, what is mankind that you are mindful of them, human beings that you care for them?" (Psalm 8:3-4). He is always and only good, caring, just, pure, right, and wise. And He wants to talk to you! He wants to hear you pray. He wants to speak to you in prayer. He wants a personal relationship with you.

It is easy to neglect prayer—even though Scripture is clear that we should pray. And though we are often reminded to pray, we think of prayer as a last resort instead of a first response. What would happen if we made the conversation of prayer part of our everyday life? What if we began to fill our days with moments of pausing, and voicing a quick prayer of praise, thanks, and petition to God? In the car on the way to work, between appointments, in the hustle and bustle of a busy day and in a quiet moment before we sleep— all of these can and should be places of prayer. Any place, any simple second in our lives can be converted from secular to sacred when we focus our heart on God and pray. His Spirit will communicate with us if we pray. The Bible says, "Seek the Lord and His strength; Seek his face evermore!" (1 Chronicles 16:11). No matter where we find ourselves, God is always ready and willing to help when we seek Him.

Prayer creates intimacy with God. Prayer isn't magic words we say to get God to do what we want. Instead, prayer is the basis for our relationship with God. Seeking His face. Loving Him. Trusting Him. When we pray, He listens and hears our hearts as well as our words—because He loves us so much. Prayer helps me see God's plan for my future, and prayer helps me trust Him for what I cannot see. Prayer helps me realign my heart, strengthen my spirit, and declare my dependence on the Father. The more I walk out my relationship with God, the more I realize that I don't pray to change God—I pray to change me.

In prayer, we learn to cooperate with God, instead of working against Him. Jennifer Kennedy Dean, the author of *The Praying Life*, said, "Prayer is the means by which you will be freed from your earth-bound, time-bound thinking to participate in eternity." It's true; we learn to see with spiritual eyes when we spend consistent and quality time in prayer. "So we fix our eyes not on what is seen, but on what is unseen. For what is seen is temporary, but what is unseen is eternal" (2 Corinthians 4:18). God is calling each of us to a personal prayer lifestyle. The only way you can be ready for *today* or *tomorrow* is to prepare in prayer.

Opening prayers. I have made it a habit to invite God to be in charge of each day before I get out bed in the morning. When my eyes open, I simply say, "God today belongs to you, help me live for you today."

Quiet time prayers. Set aside time each day to have a conversation with God. I prefer the morning before the day gets going. Another time of day might be best for you. Be sure to set the time like an unbreakable appointment. Praise and thanksgiving are powerful ways to begin the conversation with God. Some people find that writing their prayers in a journal is a way to stay focused on the Lord. Another powerful prayer tool is to pray Bible verses aloud— using God's words to honor, praise, and petition Him. Discover what helps you become a praying Christian. Speak to God about what is on your mind and heart. "God help me on the job today. Be with my kids as they have tests at school. Help me make a difference for someone else today." Whatever is on your mind, make it a prayer. Set aside time. Make an appointment. Tell Him how you feel. Thank Him. Praise Him. Ask Him for guidance. Then listen, allowing His Holy Spirit to speak words of peace and promise. If you are beginning, start with a few minutes, you'll be surprised at how quickly your time will grow.

Daily prayers. Make it a practice to say prayers throughout your day. If a coworker shares a family problem, pray a sentence prayer in that moment. If your spouse voices a concern, stop whatever you are doing and pray together. If you feel overwhelmed, ask God for peace to calm your mind and spirit. If you are going into an important presentation at work, voice a prayer asking for wisdom and clear words. Make your day an ongoing conversation with God.

Closing prayers. End your day with prayer, recognizing how He was present with you during the day and thanking Him for whatever happened today.

Prayer invites God into your moment. Preparation by praying is key to your tomorrow. So whether you are building Legos, building a business, building a marriage, building a family, or building your future, call out to your Father. He is ready to help.

The Lord is near to all who call upon him, to all who call upon him in truth (Psalm 145:18).

Chapter 2

Preparing your Perspective

You have to see it before you see it.

*It's not what you look at that
matters, it's what you see.*
~Henry David Thoreau

SHE RAN OUT THE DOOR AT FULL SPEED!
She should be in the Olympics! Our daughter Lauren was
at the pediatrician's office for a regular visit, which included
a round of shots. These were the regular immunizations
required for school, important and preventative. When the
nurse announced that it was time for the shots, Lauren got
nervous. Her heart rate went up. She started sweating. Fear
set in. What happened next was incredible. As the nurse
opened the door to bring in the tray with the pre-loaded
needles, Lauren saw her chance and ran out of the room.

It was a like a jailbreak. She didn't know where she was going. She didn't care where she was going. Anywhere was better than in that room with that nurse. She ran down the hall, around the office, and through the waiting room. My daughter ran away that day because she didn't know what I knew. She had no idea that those shots, though momentarily painful, were necessary. She couldn't see with my parent perspective, which understood that the shots would keep her from getting sick. She missed the big picture.

Don't we do that with our Heavenly Father? We run out of the room because we cannot see from His perspective.

How we see matters. Our perspective as we view our past influences our future. Whether we see our pain (past or present) as a hitching post that holds us back or a guidepost that moves us forward is often a matter of perspective and impacts our actions and feelings. We will either move on or camp in the pain. Our perspective on God either stimulates our faith or stifles our ability to trust Him. Our perspective on others determines the depth of our relationships and our emotional openness. It comes down to our perspective.

Perspective is how we view any situation. According to the dictionary, the word perspective has a Latin root meaning *look through,* and all the meanings of perspective have something to do with looking. Seeing through a certain kind of eyes.

Spiritually, we need to see everything through the divine viewpoint of God. He sees the beginning from the end. He sees the future. He sees the past. His viewpoint is clear. With our finite and limited eyesight, we can only see our current situation, but we can always trust that God sees it all.

Yesterday's viewpoint will not be enough for tomorrow. When Israel crossed the Jordan River into the Promised Land, their lives changed in drastic ways. Their perspective had to change to embrace their tomorrow. One big change was that they no longer had manna to eat. Manna was a white wafer that fell from the sky each morning. (See Exodus 16:4.) They made bread and cakes that sustained them while they lived in the barren desert. Imagine—six days a week for 40 years, the manna appeared. Their parents had been set free from slavery in Egypt, and God provided what they needed. Not one person in the nation could remember a day when they didn't have manna. They didn't have to do anything to get it. God baked it in heaven and sent it to them every morning. Now, in the Promised Land, they would have fruits and vegetables to eat because the inhabitants of the land cultivated fields and grew crops. In the desert, God took care of them because they couldn't take care of themselves. Now they were stronger, which called for a change in perspective. They would learn to farm the land, harvest the crops, pick the produce, and eat it. From gathering the food that God made for them, they moved on to possess the land.

These changes are called maturity. Raising kids is like this. Babies can do nothing except look cute. They are helpless, and then they grow, and we are proud when they accomplish something new. But what is cute behavior at six months old is not cute at 25 years old. As children grow, our expectations change. As they get older, they learn to feed and dress themselves. As they age chronologically, we expect them to grow in responsibility. Our Heavenly Father calls us to grow and mature as we walk with Him. God's people would never possess the promise of God until they came to maturity—and neither will you. Move beyond an immature faith and grow to believe God at a new level today. You and I are called by God to develop a divine viewpoint.

We don't always see our situation from heaven's side. On one occasion, the prophet Daniel prayed for more than 21 days, and he felt God wasn't listening and didn't care about his pleas. Then an angel appeared to Daniel saying that God had heard Daniel's prayers on the first day and had sent an answer. However, the answer was delayed by a battle in the heavenly realm. (See Daniel 10.) If I had been Daniel and viewing the situation with my human perspective, I might have thought God had forgotten me. But God works for us in the physical and spiritual realms. Many times He is working even when we cannot see it. We must see beyond what our natural eyes tell us, we must learn to see with the eyes of faith. A faith perspective is a God perspective. When we get a perspective like God's, we will be ready for our future.

God's vision is beyond anything we can see. I see time as a ticking clock and think that I can't wait any longer. He sees time in the continuum of eternity and knows that what seems long to me is but a fraction of the eternal timeline. I see trouble and trials from the vantage point of misery, pain, and failure, but God sees trials as a way to help me become strong and mature. I make plans, and I want to hurry to complete them, but God sees my plans as small compared to His glorious ideas for my future.

God's thoughts are beyond anything we can think. "'For my thoughts are not your thoughts, nor are your ways my ways,' says the Lord. 'For *as* the heavens are higher than the earth, so are my ways higher than your ways, And my thoughts than your thoughts'" (Isaiah 55:8-9). God cares about the large and small details. Consider creation. From enormous caverns to the tiniest flower, He is watching and caring. He cares about every detail of your life, too. We can develop a God viewpoint if we face each day trying to see through God's eyes.

Our perspective changes when we seek God. Pay attention to what you see after you pray because prayer develops eyes of faith. When you face a circumstance that you don't understand or when you think there is no hope, trust Him. Tell Him you don't understand and that you know He has placed this situation in your life for a reason. Tell Him you will trust Him even if you can't see why because you know His divine viewpoint is bigger and broader than yours.

So stay in the room and trust Him. Don't run for the door, because when you run from God, you are running away from your healer, your provider, and your protector. Whatever is happening in your life, His perspective is always best and you can believe that He wants only the best for you.

Open my eyes, that I may see
(Psalm 119:18).

Chapter 3

Prepare your Position

When you are ready, you are ready.

*The secret of success is to be
ready when your opportunity comes.*
~Benjamin Disraeli

I QUIT THE SOCCER TEAM! I was 6-years-old and along with my twin brother decided to play soccer in the community sports league. We signed up and showed up, but I found out there was more to the game than I thought. The coach put me on defense so I was supposed to stay back and defend the goal. My problem was that I wanted the ball too badly to stay where I should. The coach yelled from the sidelines for me to stay in place. He encouraged me at halftime to remain in my position. He patiently explained why I should not run after the ball. His coaching never got through my 6-year-old sensibility. I found myself chasing

31

the ball regardless of my assignment. In my young mind, being in position wasn't nearly as fun as running around the field. Our team lost because our defense was so poor. We lost because I refused to stay in position. It was my first, and also my last, season of soccer. I would have to learn the lesson of position another way.

Are you in position spiritually? I know God wants to bless your life, touch your future, and meet your every need. Are you in position to receive what God is sending your way? Or are you like me on the soccer field, running around chasing something? Our emotional, physical, and mental choices place us in position to receive His blessings. And our position determines which blessings we receive. We position ourselves by lining up with God's Word. When we follow His principles, we are ready with open hands to receive His blessings into our lives.

Don't expect to receive blessings in any area of your life if you are unwilling to walk in obedience. You will never win the soccer game without listening to the coach. And you won't win the game of life without listening to the voice of God. If you refuse to obey God's directions about giving money, don't expect financial rewards. If you don't follow God's commands about love, kindness, and forgiveness in relationships, don't complain because your friendships and family don't get along with you. If you are unfaithful in your marriage or your job, you are not positioning yourself for God's best.

Joshua challenged God's people to get in position for God's blessings. On the day that Israel crossed the Jordan River into the Promised Land, they celebrated the Passover. This celebration was a way to remember how God rescued the nation from slavery in Egypt. Moses faced the mighty Pharaoh repeatedly telling him to let God's people go from the tyranny of slavery. Pharaoh refused, and God sent ten plagues. Pharaoh remained stubborn until the last and worst plague. On that night, the angel of death entered the land of Egypt, and every first-born child and animal were slain. Except in the land of Goshen where Israel lived— because Israel followed God's redemptive plan. They sacrificed a spotless lamb and painted the blood over the doorways to their homes. When the angel saw the blood, he passed over that house and spared them from death. God's people were protected. The next day, Pharaoh allowed Israel to leave Egypt. Through Moses, God showed His people the position they needed to be in to be delivered. Through Joshua, they remembered that lesson and positioned themselves to inherit the long-awaited promise.

Your friends can help you stay in position or knock you out of position. Avoid those who are negative and who are doubters. Attitudes are contagious and their attitudes will affect your relationship with God. It is impossible to stay positive when all the influences in your life are negative. A complaining attitude will hold you back from receiving from God. Don't take my word for it; read 1 Corinthians 10:10 to see how complaining was one of the five sins that kept a whole generation from walking into God's promises. The character qualities of the people in your inner circle forecast the direction of your life. If you look at your five closest friends and do not like what you see, it's time to get some new friends. Choose to surround yourself with people who are following God with all their heart, committed to God's way, and passionate about God's plan. When you are struggling in your journey, they will lift you up and encourage you to keep going. That's what a great friend is for. These are the kinds of relationships that keep us in position.

Positioning yourself for tomorrow means dealing with your past. Our relationship with our past includes both letting go and embracing. Let go of what enslaved you, and let the Lord rescue you from the pain and difficulty of your past. But remember and cling to the moments when God intervened, liberating you from problems. God is bigger than our obstacles and even when our past circumstances seem huge, His name is above all. Remember who He is and what He has done. The Bible says, "Some *trust* in chariots, and some in horses; But we will remember the name of the Lord our God (Psalm 20:7). "I will remember the works of the Lord; Surely I will remember Your wonders of old. I will also meditate on all Your work and talk of Your deeds (Psalm 77:11-12).

These moments of God's intervention become anchors for a lifetime. Remember these five important facts about how God has been with you in the past.

1) God is bigger than any challenge I face.

2) God set me free, so I could conquer the land.

3) God has the power to do what I cannot do.

4) God has prepared a future for me.

5) God did not bring me this far to leave me now.

We must never let go of these anchors. Hear Him. (See Romans 10:9 and Hebrews 11:6.) Join Him wherever He is at work. Follow His still small voice even if you have doubts. Stay on His team and in the end, you will see the victory. Stay in position and get ready because God is about to do something great in your life.

I have come that they
may have life and that they
may have it more abundantly
(John 10:10 NKJV).

Chapter 4

Prepare your Participation

Go! Go! Go!

*Even if you are on the right track, you will get
run over if you just sit there.*
~ Will Rogers

JUST JUMP ALREADY! It was easy for my brother
to say those words. He wasn't the one standing on top of a
boulder with a 4-story drop to the surface of the lake. But I
was standing there, and I felt like I was perched on the edge
of a mile-high skyscraper. My heart was pounding. My blood
was pumping. Everyone was watching. And the voices in my
head were arguing.

Ever been there? We all have.

I had done everything in the process of getting ready to jump. I swam to the sheer shoreline. I scaled the rock face. I climbed the boulder that stood above the lake. I balanced myself on the edge of the cliff. And now there was only one thing left to do—jump. The difference between a jumper and non-jumper is found in the simple act of jumping. *Will you jump? Will you take the step? Will you take action?* If you do, it's a long way down. If you don't, the descent of defeat is center-stage for everyone to see as you climb down instead of taking the plunge. Either way, everything leads to that moment. Jump or don't jump; it's your choice.

Preparation leads to participation. That's the way it is with God. Preparation in prayer, perspective, and position lead to an action point. When you've done all you can do, it is time to join the battle, going to work where God is at work and embracing what He has planned. Participation means believing God regardless of what anyone else thinks, or how high the boulder is.

Joshua challenged the people with a "go-moment." After they were set free from bondage. After wandering in the wilderness. After the miracles that God performed on their behalf. After they learned to fight and defend themselves against their enemies. After they dealt with moments of doubt and unbelief. Finally, all the preparation came down to a choice whether to obey what God said or not. God commanded them to go. He wanted them to cross the river.

He was ready for them to embrace the future, but the choice was theirs to make. It was up to the people to take the step. It was their decision to cross into the land. It was their choice to participate in God's direction for their lives. The same is true of us. God loves us and wants the best for us, but we must choose to participate in His plan.

We all face "go-moments" in our walk with Christ. We may be mocked or dismissed, but when we are prepared, we know that Jesus is real and involved in our lives. We may not be able to explain it thoroughly, but we know Him because we are equipped. C.S. Lewis said, "I know God is not a figment of my imagination because He is nothing like I would have imagined Him to be." If we could explain Him completely, He would be limited to what we could explain. But I have good news. We don't have to understand everything about God to obey Him. Jackson Senyonga once said, "God is not here to be explained. He is here to be believed." In our journey of faith, all of us will face moments where we must choose to believe what we cannot see.

Jesus told us to go into the world. (See Matthew 28:19-20.) There are four characteristics of a "go-er."

> First, a "go-er" resists the temptation to process and filter God's Word. Stand on the truth without fear of public opinion. Sometimes when you are right, you need not explain.

Second, a "go-er" develops a strong trust in God, understanding that where God guides, He provides.

Third, a "go-er" chooses uncertainty with God over certainty without Him.

Fourth, a "go-er" considers the price of *not* going higher than the challenge of going.

Going means taking action. As I look at my life, I see those times when I knew to obey but didn't do it. Sometimes, I simply chose to disobey God's still small voice. Have you ever said something that you really regretted? Worse yet have you ever done it when you knew better? I have. I was in a meeting with a group of people when a person's name came up in the conversation. I had some issues with this person, and we really did not get along. I knew that God was telling me to be quiet, but I talked anyway. Sound familiar? I opened my big mouth and shared exactly what I thought, and none of it was good. I was negative, critical, and mean-spirited. The room was totally silent. I mistakenly thought that I would feel better after "letting it out." I was wrong. I told myself that I was "just telling it like it is." I excused my behavior to myself. But God would hear nothing of it. I knew that the Holy Spirit had warned me, and I just blew past the warning sign and kept going.

After the meeting ended, God convicted me of what I said and how I said it. I repented. I really was sorry. I had been immature and wrong. To help me learn my lesson, the Holy Spirit instructed me to personally speak with every person that was there in the meeting and apologize for my words. One hour and several humiliating phone calls later, it was done. I still remember the Lord speaking to my heart when I hung up the last phone call. He asked, "wouldn't it have been easier if you just listened and obeyed in the first place?" Boy, was He right. You never go wrong obeying God's voice.

At other times, I procrastinated. I decided to do what God wanted, just not right now. Or I waited, thinking I might get around to it. Then weeks became months and months became years and years became decades. Delayed obedience is disobedience. The best time to obey God is yesterday, and the next best time is today. Don't leave it undone.

Participating in God's calling requires me to leave some attitudes behind. Attitudes are patterns of the mind that need to be changed or renewed. I may need to change the way I think before anything at all will change. We are often captured by *stinkin' thinkin'* which sees problems as bigger than God's power. We do not naturally think like God, but we can change those bad thought patterns.

Paul wrote, "Finally, brethren, whatever things are true, whatever things are noble, whatever things are just, whatever things are pure, whatever things are lovely, whatever things are of good report, if there is any virtue and if there is anything praiseworthy—meditate on these things

(Philippians 4:8). You will find that when you focus on God and His Word, your attitude will be more like His.

There are habits that interfere with my ability to go. Some habits are sin habits. Sin is a habit or pattern of behavior that needs to be removed as we mature in our walk with Jesus. Sin is luggage you just cannot afford to carry on your journey. If there are habits and behaviors in your life right now that you know are against God's will and His Word, the answer is to repent, ask Him to forgive you, and then count on His help to make the changes needed in your life. God often delays our journey until He has done a work in us. This is why His people took so long to get to the Promised Land. God was doing a work in them first, so He could do a work through them. The same is true for us. Let God clean out anything that doesn't belong in your life, and you will be ready to take on tomorrow.

Sometimes it's not just about sin. I have found that some choices that are not over the sin boundary just are not profitable for the journey. A habit of complaining needs to be changed to a new habit of praise. Maybe you have allowed a habit such as watching mindless TV to dominate your life. It's time to replace that with new habits such as reading the Bible or serving your community. Ask God to help you remove any habits that are unproductive or harmful for your future.

Emotional pain can also block us from continuing the journey into God's will for our lives. One of the most harmful emotions that plagues Christians is unforgiveness, which is a pattern in the spirit that needs to be removed. Holding on to the pain of what someone said or did will hurt you. Jesus has great compassion for all you have walked through, but He knows that if you forgive others, you will be the one who becomes free. Forgiveness is not about who is right or wrong. It is about who is free. We must choose to let God be the judge alone. You and I were never meant to carry unforgiveness. It is radioactive to the soul. It will eat away at your faith, destroy your joy, and rob you of love. Someone once said, "forgiveness is setting the captive free, only to discover you were the one behind bars." So whatever the issue, whatever the reason, whatever the circumstance— forgive. Let God do surgery on your heart so you can be free.

When I was a boy, I climbed the wooden fence behind our house and got a splinter in my palm. It hurt—really bad. I tried and tried, but I couldn't get the splinter out. It was broken off beneath the skin. I didn't tell my dad because I knew it would hurt when he tried to dig it out. I thought I could handle the issue myself. I hid my hand from dad for about a week and a half. I used my left hand for everything because my right hand was completely useless. The situation went from bad to worse when the minuscule splinter had become a quarter-sized green infection in my hand. Finally, I couldn't hide the problem anymore. My dad noticed my left-hand switch and investigated with the skill of a district attorney. He took one look at my infected hand and began searching for needles. He heated the needle in the fire on the stove and said, "This is going to hurt a little bit." Then he punctured the wound. I screamed, "You're killing me!" But he got the splinter out, and a few days later my hand was healed.

Dad acted out of love even though he knew it might hurt me temporarily. He understood that the splinter had to come out, or it would get worse. God doesn't want the pain of your past or the misery of unforgiveness to fester in you. He will help you remove it. Will it hurt? Probably. But the pain will bring healing.

Participation with God requires that we don't hide our feelings and pain from Him. We can allow something small to become huge because we didn't take it to Him in the first place. I needed what my father did because I need the use of my hand. Participation with God means we give Him everything—even the annoying, uncomfortable parts of our life.

When we have done everything and it's time to jump, we must take action. Jump, believing that God has your back. Jump, believing that God's plan is best and He will see you through. Don't climb down from the edge and miss the thrill of the jump. And like when I jumped from a boulder on the side of a lake, someone else will be inspired to start his or her climb to the top.

Prepare yourself for tomorrow the Lord will do
wonders among you
(Joshua 3:5).

Today

*Encourage one another day after day, as long
as it is still called, "Today"
(Hebrews 3:13).*

Living for Jesus requires us to be prepared.

Every action of preparation will give us great benefit both
today and for the future. As we have considered how today
is a time of preparation, we have discovered some significant
questions we must ask ourselves if we are to be prepared.

1) What needs to go?

Just as God required Israel's men to cut away the
flesh (See Joshua 5:1-9.) in circumcision, He asks
us to remove the desires, lusts, and failures of the
flesh so we can pursue the spiritual blessings He has
arranged for us.

2) What needs to stay?

Israel continued the Passover celebration when they entered the Promised Land because it was a reminder of God's redemption and power. (See Joshua 5:10-11.) When we remember how God has intertwined Himself into our life journey, we know we can trust Him for our future.

3) What needs to change?

Israel began a new lifestyle when they left the wilderness and entered the Promised Land (See Joshua 5:12.) They were now more mature and able to feed themselves from crops they planted. They were strong enough to face obstacles like warring armies and fortified cities. They were no longer children wandering the desert. Now they were the mighty people of God showing the world that Jehovah was God. As we prepare to be all God wants us to be, we will change and mature as Christ followers.

When we pray, we match our will to God's. When we change our perspective to His divine viewpoint, we see His strength and love. When we place ourselves into position with Him as our leader, He will show us the way. Then we can join with Him wherever He is at work.

Section 2

Embracing Tomorrow

The Future

The story from the book of Joshua about Israel teaches us about embracing God's future.

> Then Joshua rose early in the morning; and they set out from Acacia Grove and came to the Jordan, he and all the children of Israel, and lodged there before they crossed over. So it was, after three days, that the officers went through the camp; and they commanded the people, saying, "When you see the ark of the covenant of the LORD your God, and the priests, the Levites, bearing it, then you shall set out from your place and go after it. Yet there shall be a space between you and it, about two thousand cubits by measure. Do not come near it, that you may know the way by which you must go, for you have

not passed *this* way before." And Joshua said to the people, "Sanctify yourselves, for tomorrow the LORD will do wonders among you" (Joshua 3:1-5).

At this point in the story of the nation of Israel, Joshua and God's people are entering into new territory. It is a new season. A fresh start. The new territory is God's promised place. It is called the Promised Land. That place is a new future, a new home, and a new inheritance.

Joshua gave the people instructions, "Sanctify yourselves, for tomorrow the Lord will do wonders among you" (Joshua 3:5). They had been wandering in the wilderness, but now it was time to change the focus to tomorrow—to shift gears.

When I was a kid, my dad taught me to drive a stick shift car. Like any good Texas boy, I began at age 12, just as soon as I could reach the pedals. Dad explained, "There are three pedals: the clutch, the brake, and the gas." Then he pointed out the gear shift and steering wheel. He showed me how to let the clutch out while pushing the gas pedal in—the action that made the car move. I pushed the clutch as far as my leg would reach. Then I popped the clutch while pushing the gas as far as it would go. The car leaped into action, and suddenly we were going way too fast and the tachometer was in the red zone. Dad yelled, "Shift the gear!"

Not shifting will damage the engine. Shifting without engaging the clutch will strip out the transmission. We must shift when driving, and we must learn to shift in life. It is time for you and me to shift gears because we won't get where we need to go unless we shift. We face situations every day that call for us to shift—a job change, a child leaves for college, marriage, the birth of kids or grandkids. These circumstances call for us to shift gears, to walk into a new tomorrow that is different than today.

Joshua and the people were about to cross over the Jordan River into the Promised Land. This moment was pivotal—a moment when they needed to embrace what God had arranged. And Joshua declared to the people that God was about to work wonders among them.

As long as we breathe, God has arranged a future for us. We may think we have disqualified ourselves and that we have compromised too much or made mistakes or acted in rebellion, but God is not finished with us.

Each morning, we can turn the page and start fresh because God wants to show up and intervene in our lives. Walking into the future may seem scary, but we must make the choice to move forward. And the changes that are awaiting us in the future are God-ordained and part of His plan.

God's miracle power is ready to work in your life. If you don't shift your thinking to tomorrow, you may stall out where you are and continue to live in yesterday.

Chapter 5

Tomorrow Has Blessings

Joy is the serious business of heaven.
~ C.S. Lewis

SHE ALWAYS LOVED PEARLS! That was one thing I learned about my wife Andrea. It's not that she doesn't appreciate diamonds. It's not that she isn't fond of gold. But to my wife, pearls are the adornment of class. They are the pinnacle of style. So I was determined to place a strand of the real-deal-authentic pearls around her neck for Christmas one year. The problem? Money was hard to come by in the early years of our marriage, and pearls cost money. So I made a plan. For six months I scrimped and saved, stealthily squirreling away a dollar at a time. I saved change. I skipped lunch. And at the end of what seemed like a marathon, I broke the piggy bank and headed to the jewelry store. The jeweler was a friend, and he helped my pick out the perfect strand—not too long and not too short. The pearls were the perfect color and the perfect size. They would be the "pièce de résistance." I left that store with an empty wallet and a full heart. It was one great Christmas day in the Booth house. Andrea was over-the-top surprised, and I was full of joy. "How were you able to afford such an expensive gift?" she asked.

"I thought of this moment months ago, and you are worth it," I answered with a smile.

Your tomorrow has blessings ready for you. They are gifts that God has dreamed up in advance. God has already set up opportunities, connections, and unexpected blessings. He thought of you before you were here. He planned ahead. He laid out a plan for your future that includes surprise moments designed to take your breath away. His plan is for you to grow up spiritually and for you to be blessed.

Each day we have a choice to pursue God's best for our lives—or not. How we handle each new day is determined by how we see God. Do we see Him as the living God who wants to bless us? Our viewpoint determines how we respond. Our response determines if we realize our potential.

If we see blessing as being only financial, we have missed God's heart. Blessing is much more than money. There are two words in the Bible translated blessing. One is Hebrew and the other is Greek. The Hebrew word is *barak* found in the Old Testament and represents God's benefits given to a person. He began in The Garden with Adam and

Eve as He blessed them so they would multiply and He filled The Garden with every good thing. The Greek word *eulogos* is used in the New Testament and means to speak words of encouragement and approval over a person. What a great picture of our Heavenly Father. He is right now in heaven speaking encouragement and approval over our life and future.

God stands at this moment in time looking over your tomorrow. He sees you, He sees what is in store for you, and He begins to set up blessings for you along your path. "For we are his workmanship created in Christ Jesus for good works, which God prepared beforehand that we should walk in them" (Ephesians 2:10). He is planting blessings for the journey in front of you. They are expressions of His Father-heart for you. They are reminders that He really does see the end from the beginning. They are the encouragement to keep going. God's future always includes blessings.

God has always been about blessing His people. As Israel began their move into the Promised Land, they saw that it was a good place. The land produced super-fruit and was referred to as the land of milk and honey. Israel didn't have to build new cities because they were already built. Crops were already growing, so there was no need to dig a garden or plow a field or plant a crop. God had prepared the land long before they arrived. He had allowed others who occupied the land to do this work so the blessing of crops and the shelter of cities would already be there when Israel arrived. This pattern is exactly how He works for us. There are blessings in the journey ahead. Some may be hidden from me, and I don't know where or what they are, but He knows.

God not only knows it all, but He is also in control of it all. The theological term is the sovereignty of God. The Bible says, "I make known the end from the beginning, from ancient times, what is still to come. I say: My purpose will stand, and I will do all that I please" (Isaiah 46:10). He is unmatched and unparalleled in power. Man is not His equal, and neither is Satan. He is unlimited in beauty, grace, majesty, and supremacy. He alone is in control. Remember, He is the same God who spoke the world into being, and He has your future in His hands.

Moving into God's future may require us to walk through some situations we did not expect or choose. Our journey may include illness, tragedy, or fear, but we can take it all to Jesus and trust it all to Jesus because His power is strong enough for our current difficulties and our future. Max Lucado said, "Let God's grace dethrone your fears. Anxiety still comes, for certain. The globe still heats up; wars still flare up; the economy acts up. Disease, calamity, and trouble populate your world. But they don't control it! Grace does."[1]

If you are facing a serious challenge in your journey today, remind yourself that God is still in control. God is still in the miracle business. God's throne of grace is available to you right now. Trust that truth.

Rabbi Jonathan Cahn told a story that illustrates how God plans our future.

> The Gedio people of Ethiopia believed in a benevolent, omnipotent, creator god named Mageno, but they spent more time appeasing an evil spirit named Sheit'an. They believed there was a distance between them and their god. One day, a man named Warrasa prayed directly to Mageno, asking Mageno to reveal himself. Warrasa saw a vision of two white men and heard a voice saying, "They will bring you a message from Mageno." Eight years passed. In 1948, two Canadian missionaries came to the town where Warrasa lived. He received them according to his vision and led 40,000 of his people to the God of the Gospel. These missionaries had no idea how God had prepared their way. Set yourself to do God's will. He'll prepare the way before you. It's true for the Gedeo people. It's true for the missionaries, and it is true for you also.[2]

My job as a Christ-follower who is preparing for the future is to expect the blessings of God. To face my future with confidence in Him alone and live in expectation and anticipation of what He will do.

God's blessings are yours because you belong to Him. When I look back at the year behind me, I see blessings that I didn't expect. I have met people I would never have met on my own. I have been places I would never have been on my own. I have experienced things I would never have experienced on my own. I have become a person I would never have become on my own. Before me are more blessings that God has arranged. I may not understand what His will is for me for the next year or decade. I cannot see the future. But God is already present in the future, and I can count on His love when I get there. Just as He loves me now and offers peace, purpose, and joy to me today, He also arranges for my tomorrow.

The same is true for you. There are great blessings in your future just waiting to be experienced, not because you are great, but because God is great. He thought of you a long time ago. He planned for you and for your destiny. He paid an incredible price, and His gifts to you are more than money could ever buy. He loves you because you are His. In fact, the Bible says that you and I are "adopted into His family" (see Ephesians 1:5).

A few months ago, as I was praying and journaling, the Holy Spirit gave me a message. I wrote furiously as He spoke to me, and when I read what was on the page, it grabbed my heart. He said, *"You are my son—I have adopted you. I have chosen you to be mine. I was not forced to take you, I chose to*

take you because my love for you is great. I will take care of you
. . . I can see tomorrow."

This message has a special place in my life because along with my twin brother, I was adopted at birth. We were two months premature and had some serious medical challenges. We were smaller than we should've been and sicker than we should've been, and we didn't have much of a chance. But my mom and dad chose us anyway. You see, if you have been born into a family and your parents love you, that is a great blessing. But being adopted is a different thing entirely. Being adopted means you have been chosen, picked out, and selected. It means that someone had a choice and they decided on you. My parents picked me even though I was sick, underdeveloped, and challenged. They were not forced to take me, they chose to take me. And God chose to take me too. Can I remind you that even in your challenges, God has chosen you too? And that is the greatest blessing of all.

And for all the guys out there, you can never go wrong with pearls. She is worth it.

> *Be anxious for nothing, but in everything by*
> *prayer and supplication, with thanksgiving,*
> *let your requests be made known to God;*
> *and the peace of God, which surpasses all*
> *understanding, will guard your hearts and*
> *minds through Christ Jesus*
> *(Philippians 4:6-7).*

Chapter 6

Tomorrow Has a Test

*Character is both developed and
revealed by tests, and all of life is a test.*
~Rick Warren

"I CAN'T WAIT FOR MY NEXT TEST!" I can't be-
lieve my son actually said those words, but he did. It sounds
foreign, doesn't it? It sounds crazy, right? I would not believe
it either except I heard it with my own ears. Why would
he say that? At 12 years old, he is pursuing a black belt in
karate. The system of study requires discipline and training.
It demands heart and skill. At regular intervals, Austin along
with his fellow students faces a belt test. It is the opportunity
to earn the next belt. He simply cannot wait to "belt up."
Belting up signifies a new level. It is the test that shows how
much he has progressed. My son is so ready to move forward
and develop his karate mojo, that he welcomes the test. I
wish we were like that about the tests we face in life. If we are
honest, not many of us ever welcome a test.

Your tomorrow is filled with blessings, but it is also filled with testings. Life's journey has obstacles. When we graduate from college or we start a new business or we begin a new position or get a promotion, there are rocks in the road ahead. Israel faced battles in the new land because they had to push out the enemies of God and take what rightfully belonged to them.

Joshua and God's people faced tests in their journey to God's Promised Land. They had to cross the Jordan River while it was in flood stage. They had to trust God's timing. They had to endure the pain of God cutting away their flesh through circumcision. Trusting God's heart meant they had to face a seemingly impenetrable walled city called Jericho with a shout as their only weapon. To do it required the people to live in an incredible place of trusting God.

We must trust God's timing. We would like to control the timing in our journey, but God is in control. I know that God is never late, but I have also found that He is rarely early. If life was up to me I would do things much differently than He does. God's timetable requires faith. He makes sure that we don't begin to rely on ourselves. It has not been an easy lesson, but I have discovered that God always has a purpose. Where I see delay, He sees an opportunity for building trust. Where I see frustration, He sees an opportunity for building patience. Where I see interruption, He sees an opportunity for a miracle. We simply cannot see everything that God sees. His timing is perfect, but we often only realize how perfect when we see through the rear-view mirror of life.

We must trust God's heart for us. He removed the flesh from Israel as a prerequisite to taking the land. Our flesh resists God and His purpose in our life. Our flesh questions God. Our flesh wars against God. Paul said, "For the flesh lusts against the Spirit, and the Spirit again the flesh; and these are contrary to one another so that you do not do the things that you wish" (Romans 5:17). We live in that tension daily. Today, removing the flesh is not a physical act but a spiritual act of removing my fleshly attitudes, my fleshly desires, and my fleshly mindsets. The physical act of circumcision points to the spiritual reality that we cannot accomplish God's will through our flesh. The New Testament says that God will circumcise our hearts (See Romans 2:29.) as the symbol of His promises to us and to assure us that He will walk with us into the future.

We must trust God's battle plan for us. I have found that His pathway to victory often does not make sense to me, but His plan is always best. I cannot see everything He can see. I cannot know everything He knows. I am limited, and He is unlimited. So if the God of the universe told His people to shout at the wall to bring victory, I should not be surprised if He speaks to me, asking me to do some things that do not compute from man's point of view. Jesus' challenges to us may seem to contradict man's reason. "Love your enemies." "Pray for those who persecute you." "Give your life away so you can find it." All of these directives can lead to great victory in your life. None of these were designed by man. But if God is on our side and we follow Him, He will bring the victory.

Blessing and testing tend to travel together throughout Scripture. Abraham's faith was tested when he was challenged to follow the promise of God and leave his home "not knowing where he was going." Joseph's character was tested when he was sexually propositioned by Potiphar's wife and later wrongly imprisoned. David's patience was tested when he was given the opportunity to kill King Saul and assume the throne. Abraham believed and was blessed. Joseph maintained his integrity and became the second most powerful ruler in Egypt. David refused to kill the king and became a great ruler in God's timing. We see the combination of tests and blessings often in life's journey. In fact, God has customized both blessing and testing to my life situation. He knows what each blessing is and why I'm receiving it, and He knows what each testing is and why I need it. He understands my talents, abilities, and heart so he knows exactly how each testing will change me and grow me.

God uses tests to reveal something to us. God sends tests to show our reliability. In the petrochemical industry, tests are made on compounds and materials to determine if that material is strong enough to do the job. Spiritual testing reveals our strengths and weaknesses by putting us under pressure. God already knows our inner character, but tests reveal the truth to us. Tests reveal the level of our commitment. Will we stand when it's not popular or easy? Will we share the gospel when it isn't politically correct? Trouble and difficulties will always introduce you to yourself.

Some situations have helped me see that I am stronger than I thought I was. I walked through it, and I am stronger. Other situations have caused me to see how much more I need to trust God and lean on Him. If you have never faced a challenge or difficulty, you will have no self-awareness, and if you have never been tested, you will never know your strength.

God uses tests to build something in us. Our trial may be for patience to grow in us. "My brethren, count it all joy when you fall into various trials, knowing that the testing of your faith produces patience" (James 1:2-3). Our trial might be for God's glory. "In this you greatly rejoice, though now for a little while, if need be, you have been grieved by various trials, that the genuineness of your faith, *being* much more precious than gold that perishes, though it is tested by fire, may be found to praise, honor, and glory at the revelation of Jesus Christ, whom having not seen you love. Though now you do not see *Him,* yet believing, you rejoice with joy inexpressible and full of glory, receiving the end of your faith—the salvation of *your* souls" (1 Peter 1:6).

To receive the blessings of tomorrow, we will face tests. There may be some difficult moments for us in the future, but God keeps us and is not absent. Endure the testing of your future with a patient and expectant heart, because God is up to good for you. It's time to belt up.

Chapter 7

Tomorrow Includes Others

*One of the most important responsibilities in the
Christian life is to care about others,
smile at them, and be a friend to the friendless.*
~James Dobson

WHERE IS "YOUR" DAUGHTER! Andrea asked me this question when she was unsuccessfully looking for our daughter, Lauren, so we could leave after a long ministry event. Incidentally, in moments like this, I am amused that she always becomes "my" daughter instead of "our" daughter, but I digress. We called her. We texted her. We searched for her. Lauren was nowhere to be found. It was insensitive, selfish, and uncaring of her to delay our departure, we complained. It was the "teenage thing" we concluded. How could she do this? After what felt like forever, Lauren emerged. She explained that she met a young lady who seemed like she needed a friend, and Lauren stopped to talk to her. They sat together in a quiet spot, and the girl poured out her heart. She shared her struggles and her pain and her tears. Lauren listened and prayed with the young lady. Lauren took an hour out of her life to focus on someone else. While we were impatient, she was patiently listening. While we thought we were starving, she was serving. While we were complaining she was encouraging. And once again I was reminded about how easy it is to get caught up in our busyness and miss God's business.

Your tomorrow is about more than you. Just as Israel was to be a light to all the nations, so are we to shine God's light on our world. I tend to be caught up in busyness and become consumed with all I must do. Instead, God calls us to reach out to others and serve others and plan our tomorrows so that we include the world around us.

Joshua was leading God's people to be a light to others. When Israel entered the Promised Land, it was more than a real-estate story or about a place to live. God's intent was to put them there in the Promised Land and bless them so much that the surrounding nations would see that God is God of all. Israel was to be a gateway for the surrounding nations to see the power and authenticity of the one true God. Other nations would see that there was something different about these people called Israel and want to know why. Why are they blessed in such an amazing way? Why do they prosper more than the rest? Why do they have peace and hope even when life is unpredictable and challenging? These are the same questions the world should be asking about God's people today. Of course, this formula falls flat if we do not walk in the faith-filled, Spirit-empowered life that God promises us.

Israel had another purpose that was beyond themselves. Ultimately God's plan was to use the nation of Israel to bring forth the Savior of the world. Jesus Christ would die on the cross for the sins of all mankind. He died so that anyone, anywhere and at any time, who puts his or her trust in Him will be saved. Israel's purpose was to point to God and provide the way for Jesus to come. Our purpose is to point the way to Jesus. God's blessing is never about you alone. It is for someone else as well.

Jesus wants all of us to make a difference for others. His calling in our life is to live for others and not just for ourselves. Jesus said, "Let your light so shine before men, that they may see your good works, and glorify your Father which is in heaven" (Matthew 5:16). Our lifestyle and words tell others about us. One man is always asked to pray before holiday meals at the office, because while most of the office doesn't follow Jesus, they can see the characteristics of God in the man. A woman is so kind and caring that the community thinks of her when they want to honor a good citizen. A couple opens their home for a neighborhood get-together and the neighbors notice the Bibles on the table and then remember that this couple goes to church every Sunday.

When your business dealings are honest and you act with integrity, others see Jesus' nature reflected in you. Consider the question, "Who do people see in you?" Let's make the reflection clear by allowing the life of Jesus to clearly show through us.

God's miracle power at work has an impact that reaches others. Joshua 3:5 says that God would work wonders for His people. Miracles. Every miracle has an impact on more than the person who received the miracle. Think about it. Jesus healed a leper, and the impact touched an entire family. Jesus met a woman at the well, and the impact touched the entire community. Jesus raised Lazarus from the dead and the impact rippled through the surrounding villages. Every encounter with Jesus has an impact on more than the person who encountered Him. Every miracle produces a story. The blind man received his sight and told his story saying, "There was a man who healed me." Every miracle and every encounter have a spillover effect.

It's true in my future as well—and yours. God has a purpose and a plan for you. Every miracle He works in your life should not end with you. Tell the story. Be bold, and let others know how great He is. Your story could be exactly what someone else needs to hear and will bring hope and life to their desperate situation.

Every person who knows Christ has a story to tell. If you've ever said, "I don't have a miracle to report," I'd like to remind you of the greatest miracle of all. That miracle is when Jesus changes your life when He becomes your Lord and Savior. When you met Him, He changed you from the inside out. Salvation is the most incredible miracle of all. Physical healing and provision are miracles, but they are temporary. The lasting miracle of salvation changes your eternity. Begin to share your story. I hope you aren't keeping it to yourself.

So walk a little slower today. Look a little deeper today. Take some time to listen to someone who needs an ear today. It's that simple. Talk to others about your faith in a fresh and non-condemning way. People will respond to your genuine love and kindness to them. And God may use you to help them receive the greatest miracle of all. And it would help if you let your mom know where you are.

Chapter 8

Tomorrow Is Not Yesterday

Faith is not knowing what the
future holds, but knowing
who holds the future.
~Anonymous

LET GO, SON! I shouted but he couldn't hear me. The noise of the engine was too loud. The sound of the wind at 30 miles an hour was too distracting. The excitement of the moment was too much for him to hear my instruction. It was Austin's first time to water ski. He was following in one of our family traditions. Both my family and Andrea's family grew up on the water. We were always around boats and enjoyed waterskiing on Lake Travis near Austin. On this particular day, it was Austin's turn to learn to ski. He was eight years old and ready for the challenge. I outfitted him with a life vest. I showed him how to hold the skis. I coached him on where to grab the handle. I prepared him for the yank of the rope as the boat accelerated. It was time.

The engine screamed as the boat pulled him from the water, and he was off. From zero to 30 miles per hour in just a few seconds—my son was skiing for the first time. I watched like any proud dad would watch—quietly congratulating myself on my coaching skills. Then he fell, and I realized I had forgotten to teach him what to do when you fall. My son held onto the rope with a death grip as the boat pulled him along.

I shouted "Let go! Let go!" but he couldn't hear me. After dragging Austin through the water as he drank the lake water, his grip finally gave way. He let go.

When he got the to the boat, I said, "Why did you hold on so long after you fell?"

He simply said, "I never heard you say to let go."

I wonder how many times our Father shouts to us to let go, but we still hang on. I wonder how often His voice is drowned out by our past pains, our current circumstances or our future fears. Maybe we need to stop for a moment right now and hear our Father's words, "Let go." Tomorrow is waiting but you must let go to embrace it.

God's people had to let go of yesterday's provision to embrace tomorrow's opportunity. Consider the changes that faced the people of Israel that day as they stood on the banks of the Jordan River. Yesterday they had received manna for food. Now they would eat vegetables. Manna was the food that God had rained down from heaven six days a week for forty years. But the day they entered the Promised Land, the manna stopped (See Joshua 5:12.) and now they would be eating food they grew in fields or gardens. God's provision for us may change in our tomorrow. He is providing in a different way in the future than He did in the past. Yesterday's manna doesn't work for us today. God has something new, bigger, better for our future.

God's people had to let go of yesterday's story to embrace tomorrow's adventure. These people had spent their entire lives in the wilderness from birth to adulthood. The skills they learned in the desert will be useless now. They were moving from tents to houses. From wandering to conquering. From walking to fighting. From dreaming to doing. No one needed to write a book titled, *How to Survive in the Wilderness.* Those skills are useless in the new land with cities and farms and cattle and populations. Tomorrow is a new day for you. It has new challenges, new opportunities, and you and I must let go of the old way and embrace the new.

God's people had to let go of yesterday's identity to embrace tomorrow's prosperity. The parents of these people had been slaves in Egypt. They were slave children.

This generation knew the stories of Egypt. They knew the terrible tales of taskmasters, brickmaking, and bondage. But their identity was changing. God did not see them as slaves but as sons. The Egypt slave mindset would not allow them to move into the Promised Land prosperity. They had to believe what God was saying about them for their future. Yesterday was over. Tomorrow was calling. The same is true for us. Yesterday is in the past. Whatever mistakes you've made or problems you've had are over. You cannot walk into your tomorrow with the baggage of yesterday.

Some of us have a yesterday trailing us—day in and day out. Those regrets. Those "if onlys." All those moments and words you wish you could change. God responds to us with words of peace and instruction. Cut the ties to yesterday, and let it go. Allow the blood of Jesus to cover your yesterday.

God is telling us to let go of yesterday. Do you need to let go? The devil is in the boat dragging you around the lake of life. He is using your past against you. Condemnation, failure, hopelessness. Sound familiar? He has been using the same strategy since the beginning. But before you drink too much of the lake of life, listen beyond the noise and the distractions—and the accusations. There is a voice speaking to you. It's the voice of your Father in heaven. He sees it all and knows it all. He knows everything you have done, and everything you have thought about doing. He knows every weak moment, bad choice, and wrong motive. The Father says to you today, let go and I will roll away your past. Let go, and I will cover your shame. Let go, and I will help you move forward.

God will help you eradicate the pain from your past and will help you move on to greater achievements for Him. You need to take some personal steps to begin the process.

Pray. Ask God to show you whatever is in your past that causes you to be stuck. Perhaps it is a relationship with a parent that was dysfunctional or harmful. God will help you put it into perspective and move on. Perhaps it is some action or behavior that carried you down to the depths of pain and sorrow. God will lift you up out of that pit.

Acknowledge. You cannot change your past. Whether it was someone who harmed you or some choice you made that caused harm, it is in the past. Acknowledge it by recognizing that it was not your fault or by admitting your mistake. When you accept the past and put it in its proper place, you can move forward.

Release. Remember that God has a plan for your future. His plans for you are always for His glory. Ask Him to reveal how your pain from your past can be a positive force in your present and trust Him for the future—even if it may contain some pain as well.

We find by losing. We hold fast by letting go.
We become something new by ceasing to be
something old. This seems to be close to the
heart of that mystery. I know no more
now than I ever did about the far side of
death as the last letting-go of all, but now I
know that I do not need to know and
that I do not need to be afraid of not
knowing. God knows. That is all that matters.
~Frederick Buechner

You have an incredible future in front of you and tomorrow is not yesterday. His plan is custom-made to fit. It is uniquely designed just for you. So let go of the rope and grab the hope.

Tomorrow

Even though Paul was in Ephesus, he wanted to travel to Corinth to see his beloved friends. But for some reason, he decided to stay in Ephesus for a while longer. He said, "For a great and effective door has opened" (1 Corinthians 16:9). Some opportunity made him change his plans. Your tomorrow is in God's hand. He will place you into the opportunity that will be the best for you.

Your choice is to trust Him and follow Him when the door opens.

There are blessings in your tomorrow. God has gone before you laying the groundwork for you to do mighty works in His name. There are also tests in your tomorrow. These trials and troubles will grow you into the person God wants you to become. These difficulties will mold you and make you as you begin to take on the characteristics of Jesus. The people in your tomorrow are waiting for you to show them the way to Jesus and for you to shower the spiritual blessings of love, joy, peace, kindness, and patience on them. Leave yesterday behind and lean into tomorrow because God is with you.

So as you face God's tomorrow for you, consider the following.

List 5 blessings God has given you so far in your journey. This list could contain answered prayers, unexpected moments, or open doors in your life. Looking back at God's faithfulness fuels our trust to believe Him for great things in the future.

Who can your tomorrow impact? Has God given you a heart for a certain group of people? Do you have a heart for teens or kids or single moms or missions? Identifying your heart-set will help to focus your future.

Are you ready for tomorrow? One thing is for sure, tomorrow will be different than yesterday. Commit now to following God regardless of the cost, and begin living the great adventure of faith. Jesus is already in your tomorrow, go discover all He has prepared for you.

> *God is not the God of the tweak;*
> *He is the God of transformation.*
> *~Garrett Booth*

Receiving Jesus Christ as Your Lord and Savior

I hope this book has helped you as you prepare for the "tomorrow" in your life. I know that you will never be all God has created you to be unless you are in a genuine personal relationship with Him. Maybe you need to receive Jesus Christ as your Savior.

A fresh start is more than a human need; it is also a spiritual necessity. One night a man came to Jesus looking for answers to his deepest spiritual desires. (See John 3:1-4.) Jesus said, "You must be born again." The man didn't get it, saying it would be physically impossible. He missed the spiritual offer Jesus made. He needed to turn away from sin and begin again by trusting Jesus as Savior.

I'd like to lead you in a prayer that is similar to the prayer that I prayed when I personally welcomed Jesus into my heart. Let me have the honor right now of sharing it with you.

Your Prayer

Dear God, I come to You and I bring me. I am doing this because I believe in Your love for me. Please help me right now. God, I believe that You sent Jesus, Your Son, to die on the cross for me. I choose to receive that truth into my life personally right now. I ask You to forgive my mess-ups and mistakes—the Bible calls them sin—through the blood of Jesus.

I open myself to a new relationship with You. I ask you to be the Lord of my life. Please change me from the inside out and make me what I could never be on my own. I invite Your Holy Spirit to fill me and lead me forward as I live for You.

Thank you for hearing my prayer. I commit myself to Jesus Christ from today until the day I see You face-to-face.

In Jesus' name, I pray. Amen.

Study and Discussion Guide

The purpose of this study and discussion guide is to help you capture the practical discoveries you are making about yourself and your walk with God as you read this book.

Each week includes **Principles for the Journey**, which are highlights from the book that will help you remember the core ideas of the chapter.

Use the **Questions for Reflection and Discussion** as your personal prayer journal or as a guide for group discussions.

These tools will enhance your journey and give you practical steps to change your life as you embrace God's tomorrow for you.

Chapter 1 – Preparing in Prayer

Principles for the Journey

➤ Prayer is simply having a conversation with God.

➤ We will never travel beyond the limits of our prayer life.

➤ Prayer creates intimacy with God.

➤ In prayer, we learn to cooperate with God, instead of work against Him.

Questions for Reflection and Discussion

Describe a time when you faced something too difficult for you. How did you respond?

_____

_____

_____

_____

_____

_____

What has been your experience with prayer? In the space below, write about a time when God answered a prayer.

_____

_____

_____

_____

_____

_____

_____

_____

On a scale of 1 (distant) to 10 (closest), how close to God do you feel right now? Where would you like to be?

Distant 1   2   3   4   5   6   7   8   9   10   Closest

Is there anything in your life that is getting in the way of you pursuing God's future for you? If so, what is it?

_____

_____

_____

_____

_____

_____

What time in your schedule will you begin to set aside to spend with God?

_____

_____

_____

_____

_____

Chapter 2 – Preparing your Perspective

Principles for the Journey

➤ Perspective is how you view any situation.

➤ Yesterday's viewpoint will not be enough for tomorrow.

➤ Growth is expected as you walk with God. It's called maturity.

➤ God's vision is beyond what we can see. His thoughts are beyond what we can think.

Questions for Reflection and Discussion

What 3 words would you use to describe yourself? Write them below.

1. _____

2. _____

3. _____

Now ask yourself if this is how God would describe you. Do you see yourself differently than God sees you? How? Why do you think there is a difference?

_____

_____

_____

_____

_____

What viewpoints from your past do you need to let go of in order to embrace tomorrow? Be specific.

_____

_____

_____

_____

What areas of your spiritual life have grown this year in your relationship with God?

_____

_____

_____

_____

_____

What is one area of your life that you would like to grow? What can you do to begin growing in that area?

_____

_____

_____

_____

_____

Chapter 3 – Prepare your Position

Principles for the Journey

➤ Blessing and obedience travel together in your life.

➤ You must position yourself to receive from God.

➤ Your friends will affect your position.

➤ Your past will affect your position.

Questions for Reflection and Discussion

What is one area of your life that you find easy to be obedient to God?

_____

_____

_____

_____

What is the blessing that comes with that area of obedience?

_____

_____

_____

_____

What is one area in which you struggle to be obedient to God?

_____

_____

What can you do right now to be obedient in that area?

_____

_____

_____

_____

Think of your 4-5 closest friends. Which of these statements describe them best?

_____Hold me back from following God most of the time.

_____Hold me back from following God sometimes.

_____Neutral—don't help or hurt my spiritual journey.

_____Help me follow God sometimes.

_____Help me follow God most of the time.

How could changing your close relationships help your spiritual life?

_____

_____

_____

_____

_____

What is one issue or hurt from your past that you feel affects you regularly?

_____

_____

_____

_____

_____

What can you do today to begin letting go of that issue or hurt?

_____

_____

_____

Chapter 4 – Prepare your Participation

Principles for the Journey

➤ Preparation leads to participation.

➤ Life has "go-moments" that we must respond to.

➤ Going means taking action.

➤ Attitudes, habits, and emotional hurt can hold you back from a "go-moment."

➤ God is a loving Father who wants to help you move into tomorrow.

Questions for Reflection and Discussion

Is there something you believe God may be challenging you to do in your life right now? Write it below.

_____

_____

_____

_____

_____

When you think about this challenge, how do you feel? (Remember God already knows)

_____

_____

_____

_____

_____

_____

_____

_____

Who could help you move forward in this area?
Do any of your personal attitudes need to change as you
move forward? What are they?

_____

_____

_____

_____

_____

Name one habit that you believe could be getting in the
way of you moving into tomorrow.

_____

_____

_____

_____

_____

Ask the Holy Spirit to search your heart for any area in
which you need to forgive another person. Now with His
help, forgive them.

Chapter 5 – Tomorrow has Blessings

Principles for the Journey

➤ Every tomorrow has blessings to go with the journey.

➤ Blessings are more than financial benefits. God wants to bless every area of your life.

➤ God's tomorrow will require you to walk through the unexpected.

➤ God's is in control, and He blesses you because you belong to Him.

Questions for Reflection and Discussion

What is your definition of a "blessing?"

_____

_____

_____

_____

_____

Looking back in your life, name three blessings that God has given you so far.

1. _____

2. _____

3. _____

Is there an area in your life that you are tempted to control rather than submit to God? Write it below.

_____

_____

_____

If you were completely convinced that God was in control of this area, would it change how you respond? Why?

_____

_____

_____

_____

_____

Write your prayer of submitting everything in your life to God in a fresh way today.

_____

_____

_____

_____

_____

_____

_____

_____

_____

_____

Chapter 6 – Tomorrow has a Test

Principles for the Journey

➤ Everyone will face tests along the journey to tomorrow.

➤ We must trust God's timing.

➤ Trusting God's heart is important when we cannot see what is ahead.

➤ God has a battle plan for every test—find it and use it.

➤ God never wastes a test. He is always building something in us through every trial.

Questions for Reflection and Discussion

Looking back, when was a time that you feel your faith was tested? Describe it below.

_____

_____

_____

_____

_____

_____

_____

_____

_____

Did you "pass" the test and move on, or "repeat" the test again?

_____

_____

_____

_____

_____

What would you do differently if you faced the same test again?

_____

_____

_____

_____

_____

Are you willing to follow God's battle plan for your test, even if it doesn't make sense to you?

_____ **Yes**   _____ **Not sure**   _____ **No**

What tests do you see coming in the future as you commit to God's tomorrow in your life?

_____

_____

_____

_____

_____

What is one step you can take today to prepare for the tests ahead?

_____

_____

_____

_____

_____

Chapter 7 – Tomorrow includes Others

Principles for the Journey

➤ Your tomorrow is about more than you.

➤ God wants you to be a light to others in your world.

➤ Every person who encounters Christ has a story to tell.

➤ Your story can reach people that someone else's story cannot reach.

Questions for Reflection and Discussion

When you think of your spiritual journey, name one person that helped you along the way and describe how they encourage you.

Person _____

How he or she helped me...

_____

_____

Choose three words that describe your life before you met Christ.

1. _____

2. _____

3. _____

Where were you when you received Jesus?

_____

_____

What changed in your life as a result of that choice?

_____

_____

_____

_____

_____

Who in your life needs to hear your story? List five people and begin to pray for an opportunity to share your story.

1. _____

2. _____

3. _____

4. _____

5. _____

Chapter 8 – Tomorrow is not Yesterday

Principles for the Journey

➤ To walk into tomorrow, you must trade yesterday's provision for tomorrow's opportunity.

➤ God has an adventure for you in tomorrow that goes beyond yesterday.

➤ God's prosperity for you is always in tomorrow.

➤ You cannot live in yesterday and embrace God's tomorrow for you.

Questions for Reflection and Discussion

As you read this book, which chapter(s) stood out the most to you? Why?

_____

_____

_____

_____

_____

What have you found most encouraging in your study? Why?

_____

_____

_____

_____

_____

What have you found most challenging? Why?

_____

_____

_____

_____

_____

What is the most important change you have made in your life as a result of your study?

_____

_____

_____

_____

_____

How can your experience with _Today and Tomorrow_ help someone else?

_____

_____

_____

_____

Acknowledgments

Thanks to my wife and kids. Your support in the process of writing this book meant the world to me.

Thanks to Grace Church Houston. Your faith and commitment make leading a joy.

Thanks to Mike Milner. Your (sometimes nagging) encouragement helped me get from an idea to a reality.

Special thanks to Karen and George Porter and Bold Vision Books. Your guidance and help in this project were present every step of the way.

About Garrett Booth

Garrett Booth preaches, teaches, and leads with a passion to see God's people empowered to live a Spirit-formed life. He pastors Grace Church Houston. Garrett and his wife, Andrea, have served in full-time ministry for more than 20 years. He is a graduate of Southwestern Assemblies of God University and holds a Master's degree in Practical Theology from The King's University, founded by Jack Hayford. Garrett and Andrea married in 1997 and have two fun-loving kids, Lauren and Austin.

Connect with Garrett @

 GarrettBooth.org

 Garrett Booth

 @garrettbooth

 @garrettbooth

About Grace Church Houston

Grace Church Houston is a non-demoninational, Christ-centered church in Houston, Texas. Located on 86 acres near Beltway 8 and Interstate 45, the worship center accommodates 10,000 people with multiple classrooms, auditoriums, a gymnasium, and a huge kids playscape.

With weekend services, mid-week services, small groups, Bible studies, Equip classes, Youth and Children's programs, and much more, Grace provides a variety of ministries and an engaging community for a diverse multi-cultural congregation.

The church is part of Grace International, a fellowship of churches serving more than 180,000 members in more than 3,000 churches in 99 nations. Grace International embraces a vision of continued expansion and growth by planting churches in the United States and around the world.

Connect with Grace Church Houston @

 gracehouston.tv

 gracehoustontx

 @gracehoustontx

@GraceHoustonTx

Connect with Grace International @

gracechurches.tv

gracechurchesglobal

gracechurchesglobal

graceinternational

(Endnotes)

1 Max Lucado, *God is With You Every Day*, Thomas Nelson, 2015. p.367

2 Jonathan Cahn, *Sapphires*, August 2016.